LAETENTUR CAELI

Bulls of Union with the Greek, Armenian, Coptic, and Ethiopian Churches

Eugenius IV,
Pope of Rome

Translated by: D.P. Curtin

Dalcassian Publishing Company

PHILADELPHIA, PA

LAETENTUR CAELI

Copyright @ 2007 Dalcassian Publishing Company

All rights reserved. No part of this publication may be reproduced, distributed, or transmitted in any form or by any means, including photocopying, recording, or other electronic or mechanical methods, without the prior written permission of the publisher, except in the case of brief quotations embodied in critical reviews and certain other non-commercial uses permitted by copyright law. For permission request, write to Dalcassian Publishing Company at dalcassianpublishing at gmail.com

ISBN: 979-8-8691-7150-4 (Paperback)

Library of Congress Control Number:
Author: Curtin, D.P. (1985-)

Printed by Ingram Content Group, 1 Ingram Blvd, La Vergne, Tennessee

First printing edition 2007.

LAETENTUR CAELI

LAETENTUR CAELI

Bulls of Union with the Greek, Armenian, Coptic, and Ethiopian Churches

LAETENTUR CAELI

BULL OF THE GREEK UNION

July 6, 1439

ECUMENICAL COUNCIL XVII AT FLORENCE

26 February 1439 - Aug. 1445

SESSION VI

Definition of the Holy Ecumenical Synod of Florence

Bishop Eugene, servant of the servants of God, to the perpetual memory of the matter.

With the consent of the undersigned, to our dearest son John Paleologus, the illustrious emperor of the Romans, and to the lieutenants of our venerable brothers, the patriarchs, and to the rest of the representatives of the eastern church.

Let the heavens rejoice and let the earth rejoice (Ps. 95:11) For the middle wall that divided the church between the west and the east was removed, and peace and harmony returned to that *cornerstone, Christ, who made both one* (Eph. 2:20), by a very strong bond of charity and peace, connecting both the wall and the perpetual bond of unity, connecting and holding it together; and after the long fog of misery and the dark and unpleasant gloom of long-standing dissension, the clear command of union dawned upon all. Rejoice also the mother church, who sees her children, hitherto at odds with one another, now returned to unity and peace; and who had previously wept most bitterly at their

LAETENTUR CAELI

separation, from their own way he returned thanks to Almighty God for their wonderful harmony with inexpressible joy. All the faithful everywhere throughout the world are to be congratulated, and those who are considered Christian by name are gathered to the mother Catholic Church. For behold, the western and eastern fathers, after a long period of dissension and discord, exposing themselves to the dangers of the sea and the land, and having overcome all their labors, came together to this sacred ecumenical council with the desire of the most sacred union and ancient charity to reintegrate the grace of grace, happiness and enthusiasm. And they were by no means frustrated in their intention. For after a long and laborious search, at last, by the mercy of the Holy Spirit, they obtained the most desired and most holy union. Who, then, is worthy to give thanks for the favors of Almighty God? (1 Th. 3:9) Who does not marvel at the riches of such divine mercy? Whose iron breast is not softened by such a greatness of divine piety? These are absolutely divine works, not invented by human frailty; and therefore, to be received with extraordinary veneration, and to be pursued with divine praise. Praise to thee, glory to thee, thanksgiving to thee, O Christ, fountain of mercies, who hast contributed so much to the Catholic Church as a good bridegroom, and in our generation you have shown the miracles of your piety, so that all your wonders may be told (Tob. 12:20). Indeed, God has given us a great and divine gift; and we saw with our eyes that many before us, when they greatly desired, were unable to look (Mt. 13:16-17).

For when the Latins and the Greeks met in this sacrosanct ecumenical synod, they used each other with great interest, so that, among other things, that article about the divine procession of the Holy Spirit was discussed with the utmost care and constant investigation. But having brought forward the testimonies from the divine scriptures and the numerous authorities of the holy teachers of the East and the West, some indeed saying that the Holy Spirit proceeds from the Father and the Son, and some others from the Father through the Son, and looking to the same intelligence in all under different terms, the Greeks indeed asserted that what they say The Holy Spirit proceeding from the Father, they do not with this mind put forward to exclude the Son but because it seemed to them, as they say, that the Latins assert that the Holy Spirit proceeds from the Father and the Son as from two principles and two breaths, they therefore refrained from saying that the Holy Spirit proceeds from the Father and the

LAETENTUR CAELI

Son. But the Latins asserted that they do not mean to say that the Holy Spirit proceeds from the Father and the Son, so as to exclude the Father from being the source and principle of the whole deity, that is, the Son and the Holy Spirit, or that what the Holy Spirit proceeds from the Son, the Son does not have from the Father; whether they posit that there are two principles or two breaths, but that they assert that there is only one principle and the only breath of the Holy Spirit, as they have hitherto asserted. And when from all this one and the same sense of truth is elicited, at last they concurred and consented unanimously in the underwritten union, holy and lovable to God, with the same sense and the same mind.

Therefore, in the name of the Holy Trinity, of the Father, of the Son, and of the Holy Spirit, by approving this sacred universal council of Florence, we define that this truth of the faith may be believed and received by all Christians, and that all may profess it.

That the Holy Spirit is eternally from the Father and the Son (Lyon II, Canon I), and has its essence and its subsisting being from the Father and the Son together, and proceeds from both eternally as if from one principle and one inspiration, declaring that what the holy teachers and fathers say, For the Holy Spirit to proceed from the Father through the Son tends to this understanding, so that by this it is signified that the Son is also the cause, according to the Greeks, indeed, according to the Latins, the principle of the Holy Spirit's subsistence, as well as the Father. And since the Father himself gave to his only begotten Son by begetting all that is the Father's, besides being the Father; This very fact, that the Holy Spirit proceeds from the Son, the Son himself has eternally from the Father, from whom he is also eternally begotten. Moreover, we define that the explanation of those words and the Son, declaring the truth by the grace and imminent necessity at that time, was lawfully and reasonably applied to the symbol.

Also, in unleavened or leavened bread of wheat, the body of Christ should be truly prepared, and the priests should prepare the Lord's body in the other, each according to the custom of his church, whether Western or Eastern.

LAETENTUR CAELI

Likewise, if truly penitents have died in the love of God, before they have satisfied and forsaken the fruits of penance worthy of their commissions, their souls may be purified by the penitentiaries after death, and, in order to be freed from such punishments, the votes of the living faithful may benefit them, that is, the sacrifices of the masses, prayers and alms and other services of piety, which are customarily performed by the faithful for other faithful, according to the institutions of the church.

And the souls of those who, after receiving baptism, incurred no stain of sin at all; even those who, after contracting the stain of sin, either in their bodies, or in their naked bodies, as has been said above, are cleansed, may soon be received into heaven (*Benedictus Deus,* Benedict XII, 29 Jan. 29, 1336), and may behold clearly God himself, triune and one, as he is, yet for the meritorious different from one another more perfectly.

But the souls of those who die in actual mortal sin, or in the original soil, will soon descend into hell, yet to be punished with disparate punishments.

Likewise, we define the holy apostolic see and the Roman Pontiff to hold primacy in the whole world, and that the Roman Pontiff himself is the successor of the blessed Peter, the chief of the apostles, and the true vicar of Christ, the head of the whole church, and the father and teacher of all Christians, and that he himself exists in blessed Peter to feed, rule, and govern the universal that the church has been given full power by our Lord Jesus Christ, as is also contained in the acts of the ecumenical councils and in the sacred canons.

Moreover, renewing the traditional order in the canons of the other venerable patriarchs, that the patriarch of Constantinople should be second after the most holy Roman pontiff, the third of Alexandria, the fourth of Antioch, and the fifth of Jerusalem, thus saving all their privileges and rights (Chalcedon, Canon XXVIII; Lateran IV, Canon V).

LAETENTUR CAELI

Given at Florence, in a public session of the synod, solemnly celebrated in the greater church, in the year of the Incarnation Sunday 1439, the day before the ninth of July, in the 9th year of our pontificate.

I, Eugene, Catholic. Bishop of the Church, thus defining I subscribed.

LAETENTUR CAELI

EXULTATE DEO

BULL OF THE ARMENIAN UNION

November 22, 1439

ECUMENICAL COUNCIL XVII AT FLORENCE

26 February 1439 - Aug. 1445

Session VIII

Bishop Eugene, servant of the servants of God, to the perpetual memory of the matter.

Rejoice in the God of *our helper, rejoice in the God of Jacob* (Ps. 80:2), all you everywhere who consider yourself a Christian by name. For behold, the Lord *remembered again in his mercy* (Lk. 1:54) and deigned to remove from his church another stone of dissension, which had been more than a thousand years old, and which had become even more ancient. *And he who makes concord in the highest* (Lk. 25:2), *and on earth there is peace for men of good will* (Lk. 2:14), granted the much-desired union of the Armenians with his ineffable mercy. *Blessed be the God and Father of our Lord Jesus Christ, the Father of mercies and the God of all comfort, who comforts us in all our tribulations* (2 Cor. 1:3-4). For the most pious Lord looks upon his church, *not only from those who are outside* (1 Tim 3:7), but only from those who are inside, and will not be tossed by small storms; and is worthy to be strengthened.

For long ago he established that great union of the Greeks with the many nations and languages of the continents, but today this same Armenian people, who have spread throughout the north and east in great numbers, has established in the same bond of faith and charity with the apostolic see. Indeed, these are so great and wonderful the benefits of divine piety, that not only for both, but not even for the other, the human intellect can give enough thanks to his majesty. Who is not greatly astonished at the fact that, in such a short time, two works so eminent, and desired for so many centuries, were so successfully accomplished in this sacred council? This has truly happened to *the Lord and is wonderful in our eyes* (Ps. 117:23). For what reason could the prudence or industry of men, unless the grace of God had both received and accomplished, been able to accomplish such and such great things? Let us constantly praise and wholeheartedly bless the Lord, *who alone does great wonders* (Ps. 135:4), we who sing with the spirit, we sing with the mind and the mouth, and with the work (1 Cor. 14:15), as far as human frailty allows, for so many gifts let us give thanks, praying and beseeching, that just as the Greeks and Armenians themselves have become one with the Roman Church, so may the rest of the nations, especially those marked with the character of Christ, and finally the whole Christian people, having extinguished all hatreds and wars, mutually rest in peace and fraternal love, and let him rejoice

But we consider the Armenians themselves to be worthy of great praise. For the first time they were gathered by us to the synod, as if ecclesiastically eager for unity, their respectable, devout, and learned orators, with a sufficient command to observe *whatever the Holy Spirit enlightened this holy synod,* from the remotest regions through the many labors of the sea which are dangers to us and this sacred They appointed a council.

We, however, with all our heart, as befits our pastoral duty, desiring to complete so holy a work, joined the fence with the speakers themselves about this holy union. And that there should not be even a slight delay in this sacred matter, we deputed from every state of this sacred council the most learned men of divine and human law, who with all care, study, and diligence went over this matter with the orators, accurately inquiring from them of their faith in the divine unity being so and the Trinity of divine persons, the humanity of our Lord Jesus Christ, and the seven sacraments of the church, and other things pertaining to the orthodox faith and the rites of the universal church.

LAETENTUR CAELI

Having therefore employed many discussions, conferences, and treaties, and after a not moderate inspection of the testimonies which were brought forth from the holy fathers and teachers of the church, and the discussion of the things which were discussed, we finally decided to expedient, lest in the future there should be any truth of the faith among the Armenians themselves. that there should be hesitation, and that they should be wise in all things to the same with the apostolic see, a union which itself would persevere stable and perpetual without any scruple, so that under a certain brief summary the truth of the orthodox faith, which the church professes on Roman premises by this decree, approving this by the sacred Florentine council, themselves We would also hand over to the speakers who agree to this.

In the first place, then, we give them the holy symbol issued by one hundred and fifty bishops in the ecumenical council of Constantinople, with that addition and to the *Son* himself as a symbol declaring the grace of truth and the urgent necessity lawfully and reasonably added, the tenor of which is as follows: *I believe* .... But this holy symbol, as It is the custom among the Latins, so we decree that it be sung or read in all the Armenian churches during the solemnities of the masses at least every Sunday and major festivals.

Secondly, we deliver to them the definition of the fourth council of Chalcedon, renewed in the fifth and later in the sixth universal councils, concerning the two natures in the one person of Christ, the tenor of which is as follows: *It would suffice ...*

Thirdly, the definition of the two wills and the two operations of Christ promulgated in the aforesaid sixth council, the tenor of which is: *Indeed, it would be enough,* and the rest, which in the very definition of the Council of Chalcedon is narrated above, follow until the end, after which it follows in this way: *And two ...*

Fourthly, since until now the Armenians themselves, past these three first synods of Nicaea, Constantinople, and Ephesus, had not held any other universal ones after that, nor the most blessed of this holy see, the ancient Leo, by whose authority the very synod of Chalcedon existed, they had gathered together, asserting that it was the platform of them, so the synod itself We instructed them that the aforementioned Leo had made a definition according to Nestorius' damned heresy, and we declared that this was a false suggestion that the Chalcedon synod and the most blessed Leo had holy and rightly defined the truth about the two natures in one person of Christ described above against the impious dogmas of Nestorius and Eutychus, and we enjoined, that the most blessed Leo himself, who was truly a pillar of faith and filled with all sanctity and doctrine, should be regarded as a saint and described in the catalog of saints by virtue of the rest, and should be venerated, and not only the said three synods, but all other universal ones lawfully celebrated by the authority of the Roman pontiff, just as let the rest of the faithful receive them reverently.

Fifthly, we reduce the truth of the ecclesiastical sacraments for the Armenians themselves, both present and future, to an easier doctrine under this very brief formula: There are seven sacraments in the new law, namely, baptism, confirmation, eucharist, penance, extreme anointing, order and marriage, which differ a lot from the sacraments of the ancient law. For they did not cause grace but imagined that it was to be given only through the passion of Christ. Indeed, they contain our grace and bestow it on those who receive it worthily. The first five of these are directed to the spiritual perfection of each man in himself, the last two to the government and multiplication of the whole church. For through baptism we are spiritually reborn; by confirmation we are increased in grace and strengthened in faith. Reborn and strengthened, we are nourished by the divine Eucharist. But if through sin we incur sickness in the soul, we are spiritually healed through penance. Spiritually also, and bodily, as the soul expedients, by extreme anointing. But through order the church is governed, and the spiritual journey is multiplied, through marriage it is increased physically. All these three sacraments are accomplished, that is to say, with things as matter, words as form, and the person of the minister conferring the sacrament with the intention of performing it, which the church does. If any of them is lacking, the sacrament is not completed. Among these three sacraments are baptism, confirmation, and ordination, which impress upon the soul an indelible character, that is to say, a spiritual mark which distinguishes it from the rest. Hence, they are not repeated in the same person. But the other four do not print the character and allow repetition.

Holy Baptism holds the first place of all the sacraments, which is the door to the spiritual life; through him we are made members of Christ and of his body the church. And when death entered the universe through the first man (Rm. 5:12), unless we are reborn of water and spirit, we cannot, as the Truth says, enter the kingdom of heaven (Jn. 3:5). The substance of this sacrament is true and natural water, and it does not matter whether it is cold or hot. Now the form is: I baptize you in the name of the Father and of the Son and of the Holy Spirit. However, we do not deny that even with those words: let such a servant of Christ be baptized in the name of the Father and of the Son and of the Holy Spirit, or: let such a one be baptized with my hands in the name of the Father and of the Son and of the Holy Spirit, but let the baptism be completed. For since the holy Trinity is the main cause from which baptism has power, and the minister who delivers the sacrament outwardly is instrumental, if the act which is exercised through him is expressed the minister, the sacrament is completed with the holy invocation of the trinity. The minister of this sacrament is the priest, who is entitled to baptize as a matter of duty; but in a case of necessity, not only a priest or a deacon, but also a layman or a woman, nay, a heathen and a heretic, can baptize, provided that he keeps the form of the church and intends to do what the church does. The effect of this sacrament is the remission of all original and actual guilt, and almost all that is due for the guilt itself; therefore, no satisfaction is required for the baptized for past sins, but those who die, before committing any fault, immediately reach the kingdom of heaven and the vision of God.

The second sacrament is Confirmation, the material of which is a chrism made of oil, which signifies the luster of conscience, and balsam, which signifies the fragrance of good hunger, blessed by the bishop. Now the form is: I sign you with the sign of the cross and I confirm you with the chrism of salvation in the name of the Father and of the Son and of the Holy Spirit. The ordinary minister is the bishop. And while a simple priest may present the other anointings, this one alone must be conferred by the bishop, because it is read of the apostles alone, whose turn the bishops hold, that they gave the Holy Spirit by the laying on of hands, as the reading of the Acts of the Apostles makes clear.

For when, he says, the apostles who were in Jerusalem heard that Samaria had received the word of God, they sent Peter and John to them, who, when they came, prayed for them that they might receive the Holy Spirit. for he had not yet come to any of them, but they had only been baptized in the name of the Lord Jesus; then they laid their hands on them, and they received the Holy Spirit (Acts 8:14-17). Instead of that laying on of hands, confirmation is given in the church. It is read, however, that on one occasion, through the dispensation of the apostolic see, for a very reasonable and urgent reason, a simple priest administered this sacrament of confirmation after the chrism had been done by the bishop. The effect of this sacrament is that in it the Holy Spirit is given for strength, just as it was given to the apostles on the day of Pentecost, so that the Christian may boldly confess the name of Christ. And therefore in the forehead, where the seat of shame is, he is anointed to be strengthened, lest he be ashamed to confess the name of Christ, and especially his cross, *which is a stumbling block to the Jews, but to the Gentiles foolishness* (1 Cor 1:23), according to the Apostle, for which reason it is signed with the sign of the cross.

The third is the sacrament of the Eucharist. And water is therefore mixed, because according to the testimonies of the holy fathers and teachers of the church presented a long time ago in a discussion, it is believed that the Lord himself instituted this sacrament in wine mixed with water; For blessed Alexander the pope says, V from blessed Peter: "In the offerings of the sacraments, which are offered to the Lord within the solemnities of the masses, only bread and wine mixed with water should be offered as a sacrifice." For in the cup of the Lord neither wine alone nor water alone should be offered, but both mixed together, because on both sides it is read that blood and water flowed from the side of Christ" (Cf. Jn 19:34) and also what is appropriate to signify the effect of this sacrament, which is the union of the Christian people to Christ. For water signifies the people according to the apocalypse: and many waters, many peoples (Reve. 17:15). And Pope Julius, who followed the blessed Sylvester, said that according to the precepts of the canon, the Sunday cup should be offered mixed with wine and water, because we see that in water the people are understood, but in wine the blood of Christ is shown; therefore, when wine and water are mixed in the cup, the people are united to Christ, and the people of the faithful, in whom they believe, are united and united. Since, then, the holy Roman church, taught by the most blessed apostles Peter and

LAETENTUR CAELI

Paul, and all the rest of the Latin Greeks, who, in the church in which the lights of all sanctity and doctrine shined, have preserved and continue to preserve the church in this way from the beginning respect for universal and reasonable differences. We decide, therefore, that the Armenians themselves should also conform to the whole Christian world in that the priests should mix a little water and, as has been said, wine in the offering cup. The form of this sacrament are the words of the Savior, with which he accomplished this sacrament. For the priest, speaking in the person of Christ, accomplishes this sacrament. For by the power of their own words the substance of the bread is changed into the body of Christ, and the substance of the wine into blood. Nevertheless, since the whole Christ is contained under the appearance of bread and the whole under the appearance of wine, the whole Christ is also under each part of the consecrated host and the separation of the consecrated wine. The effect of this sacrament, which it works in the soul when taken worthily, is the union of man with Christ. And since by grace man is incorporated with Christ and is united to his members, it follows that through this sacrament in those who receive it, all the effect which material food and drink have with respect to bodily life is increased by worthy grace, by sustaining, increasing, repairing and delighting, this sacrament as to He works a spiritual life in which, as Pope Urban says, we recall the good memory of our Savior, we withdraw from evil, we are strengthened in good, and we advance to the growth of virtues and graces.

The fourth sacrament is Penance, the substance of which are the actions of the penitent, which are divided into three parts; the first of which is the breaking of the heart, to which it belongs, that he grieves over the sin he has committed, with the intention of not sinning about the rest. The second is the confession of the mouth, to which it belongs, that the sinner should fully confess to his priest all the sins of which he has memory. The third is satisfaction for sins according to the discretion of the priest, which is done mainly through prayer, fasting and almsgiving. The form of this sacrament are the words of absolution which the priest pronounces when he says: I absolve you. The minister of this sacrament is a priest having the authority to absolve either ordinary or by commission of a superior. The effect of this sacrament is absolution from sins.

The fifth sacrament is the last Anointing, the substance of which is olive oil blessed by the bishop. This sacrament should not be given except to the sick, whose death is feared, who is to be anointed in these places, in the eyes for seeing, in the ears for hearing, in the noses for smelling, in the mouth for tasting or speaking, in the hands for touching, in the feet for walking, in the kidneys for the delight prevailing there. The form of this sacrament is this: Through this anointing and his most pious mercy, may the Lord indulge you in whatever you have transgressed by sight, and similarly in other members. The minister of this sacrament is the priest. The effect is indeed the healing of the mind and, in so far as it is useful for the soul, of the body as well. Of this sacrament the blessed James the Apostle says: *If anyone among you is sick, let him bring the priests of the church to pray over him, anointing him with oil in the name of the Lord. and the prayer of faith will save the weak and the Lord will relieve him, and if he is in sins, he will be forgiven* (Jam. 5:14-15).

The sixth is the sacrament of the Order, the matter of which is that through the tradition of which the order is conferred. As the presbyterate is handed down by the breaking of the cup with the wine and the platter with the bread. But the diaconate was by giving the book of the gospels. The subdeacon, however, by the tradition of an empty cup with an empty plate on top of it. And in the same way about others through the assignment of things pertaining to their ministries. The form of the priesthood is as follows: Receive the power to offer sacrifice in the church for the living and the dead, in the name of the Father and of the Son and of the Holy Spirit. And so, on the forms of other orders, as it is largely contained in the Roman Pontifical. The ordinary minister of this sacrament is the bishop. The result is an increase in grace, so that one can be a true minister of Christ.

The seventh is the sacrament of Marriage, which is a sign of the union of Christ and the church, according to the apostle who said: *This sacrament is great, but I say in Christ and in the church* (Eph. 5:32). The effective cause of marriage is usually mutual consent expressed in words about the present. A triple good is assigned to marriage. The first thing is to receive children and bring them up for the worship of God. The second is the faith which one spouse must keep to the other. Thirdly, the indivisibility of marriage, because it signifies the indivisible union of Christ and the Church. Although it is permissible for a

LAETENTUR CAELI

husband to divorce on the grounds of fornication, it is not right to contract another marriage, since the bond of marriage legally contracted is perpetual.

Sixthly, we present to the orators themselves that concise rule of faith issued by the blessed Athanasius, the tenor of which is as follows:

Whoever wishes to be saved must first of all hold to the Catholic faith, which, unless everyone keeps it intact and inviolable, will undoubtedly perish forever. But the Catholic faith is this, that we worship one God in Trinity and the Trinity in unity, neither confounding the persons nor separating the substance. For there is one person of the Father, another of the Son, another of the Holy Spirit, but the Father and the Son and the Holy Spirit are one divinity, equal in glory, eternal majesty.

Like the Father, like the Son, like the Holy Spirit.

Uncreated Father, uncreated Son, uncreated Holy Spirit.

Immense Father, Immense Son, Immense Holy Spirit.

Eternal Father, Eternal Son, Eternal Holy Spirit.

And yet not three eternal ones, but one eternal one.

As not three uncreated nor three immense, but one uncreated and one immense.

Likewise, the almighty Father, the almighty Son, the almighty Holy Spirit.

And yet not three almighty, but one Almighty.

LAETENTUR CAELI

Yes, God the Father, God the Son, God the Holy Spirit.

And yet there are not three gods, but one God.

Yes, the Lord, the Father, the Lord, the Son, the Lord, the Holy Spirit.

And yet there are not three masters, but one Lord.

For just as we are compelled by Christian truth to confess each and every person God and Lord, so we are forbidden by the Catholic religion to say three gods or lords.

The Father was not made, created, or begotten by anyone.

The Son is from the Father alone, not made or created, but begotten.

The Holy Spirit was neither made nor created nor begotten by the Father and the Son, but proceeding.

One Father, therefore, not three fathers.

One Son, not three sons.

One Holy Spirit, not three Holy Spirits.

And in this Trinity, there is nothing before or after, nothing greater or less, but all three persons are eternally and co-equal.

So that in all things, as has already been said above, both the unity in the Trinity and the Trinity in unity should be venerated.

Therefore, he who wishes to be saved must feel this way about the Trinity.

But it is necessary for eternal salvation to faithfully believe in the incarnation of our Lord Jesus Christ.

Faith is therefore right, that we believe and confess that our Lord Jesus Christ, the Son of God, is God and man.

God was born from the substance of the Father before the ages, and man was born from the substance of the mother in the ages.

Perfect God, perfect man, subsisting from a rational soul and human flesh.

Equal to the Father in divinity, inferior to the Father in humanity.

Although he is God and man, yet Christ is not two, but one.

But one, not by the conversion of divinity into flesh, but by the assumption of humanity into God.

One at all, not by confusion of substance, but by unity of person.

For as the rational soul and the flesh are one man, so God and man are one Christ.

He who suffered for our salvation descended to hell.

LAETENTUR CAELI

On the third day he rose from the dead.

He ascended into heaven and sits at the right hand of God the Father almighty.

From there he will come to judge the living and the dead.

At the coming of which all men must rise again with their bodies and must give an account of their own deeds. And those who have done good will enter into eternal life.

Those who are evil, into eternal fire.

This is the Catholic faith, which unless everyone faithfully and firmly believes that he cannot be saved.

The seventh decree of the consummation of the union with the Greeks, promulgated a long time ago in this sacred ecumenical council of Florence, the tenor of which is as follows: *Let the heavens* ...

Eighthly, since, among other things, it was also discussed with the Armenians themselves, on which days the festivals of the Annunciation of the Blessed Virgin Mary, the birth of the Blessed John the Baptist, and consequently the birth and circumcision of our Lord Jesus Christ and the presentation of the same in the temple or the purification of the Blessed Virgin Mary should be celebrated, enough that the truth is clear It has been revealed both by the testimonies of the holy fathers and by the custom of the Roman church and of all others universally among the Latins and Greeks, so that in such celebrities there should not be a disparity in the rite of Christians, from which the occasion of disturbing charity might arise, we decide, as consistent with truth and reason, that according to the respect of the rest of the world we The Armenians should also celebrate the feast of the Annunciation to the blessed Mary on the twenty-fifth of March, the birth of blessed John the Baptist on the

LAETENTUR CAELI

twenty-fourth of June, the nativity according to the flesh of our Savior on the twenty-fifth of December, the circumcision of the same on the first of January, the Epiphany on the sixth of the same January, the presentation of the Lord in the temple or the purification of the mother god on the second of February to solemnly celebrate

Having explained all this, the aforesaid speakers of the Armenians, in the name of themselves and of their patriarch and of all Armenians, this most salutary synodal decree with all its chapters, declarations, definitions, traditions, precepts and statutes, and all the doctrine described in it, as well as whatever the holy apostolic see and the Roman church holds and teaches, with all devotion and obedience they accept, receive and embrace. Those teachers and holy fathers whom the Roman church approves of, they themselves reverently receive. But whatever persons and whatever the Roman Church itself rejects and condemns, they themselves regard as rejected and condemned. Profiting as if by true obedience in the name of the son above, to faithfully obey the ordinances and orders of the apostolic see.

Given at Florence, in a public synodal session, solemnly celebrated in the greater church, in the year of the Lord 1439, the tenth day of December, in the 9th year of our pontificate.

LAETENTUR CAELI

CANTATE DOMINO

BULL OF THE UNION OF COPTS AND ETHIOPIANS

February 4, 1442

ECUMENICAL COUNCIL XVII AT FLORENCE

26 February 1439 - Aug. 1445

Session XI

Bishop Eugene, servant of the servants of God, to the perpetual memory of the matter.

Sing to the Lord, for I have done magnificently; announce this in all the earth; Rejoice and praise, O habitation of Zion, for great is the holy Israel in your midst (Is. 12:5-6). Surely the church of God should sing and rejoice in the Lord for this great magnificence and glory of his name, which the most merciful God has deigned to work on this day. Indeed, it behooves us to praise and bless our Savior with all our hearts, who daily accumulates new growths in his holy church. And although his favors to the Christian people are many and great at all times, which show his immense love towards us more clearly, if we look accurately at what and how much divine clemency he has deigned to do in these last days, we shall surely be able to judge that in our time there are more and greater that his gifts of charity had existed from many backward ages. For behold, not yet exactly three years ago, in this holy ecumenical synod, the most salubrious union of the three great nations was effected by our Lord Jesus Christ, by his tireless piety to the common perpetual, which brought about so abundantly the joy of all Christianity. Wherefore it was done, that almost the whole of the east, which adores the glorious name of Christ, and not a small portion of the north, after long dissensions with the holy Roman church, have

LAETENTUR CAELI

now come together in the same bond of faith and charity. First, indeed, the Greeks and those who are under the four patriarchal seats, many peoples, nations, and nations on the continent, then the Armenians, a nation of many peoples, and today the Jacobins, a great people even throughout Egypt, are united apostolically to the holy see.

And since nothing is more pleasing to our savior, the Lord Jesus Christ, than mutual love between men, and nothing can be more glorious to his name and more useful to the church than that Christians should unite in the same purity of faith in all the differences that have arisen among themselves, it is right that we should all sing for joy and rejoice we owe it to the Lord, whom divine mercy has made worthy, that we may see such magnificence of the Christian faith in our days. Therefore, with the greatest enthusiasm, we announce this great event throughout the Christian world, so that just as we are filled with indescribable joy for the glory of God and the exaltation of the church, so we may make others share in such joy, so that we may all magnify and glorify God with one mouth (Rm. 15:6) and his to his majesty, as befits, the great daily thanks which we give for so many and so many and wonderful favors, which in this age he bestowed upon his church. And since he who carries out the work of God diligently, not only expects merit and retribution in heaven, but also among men the great glory and praise which he deserves, our venerable brother John, the patriarch of the Jacobins, the most avid of this holy union, should be deservedly praised and exalted by us and the whole church and We judge him worthy of the common favor of all Christians with his whole nation. For he was incited by us through our orator and letters to send an embassy to us and this holy synod, and to unite himself and his nation in the same faith with the Roman church, his beloved son Andrew, a native of Egypt, abbot of the monastery of Saint Anthony in Egypt. in which Saint Antony himself is said to have lived and died, not moderately educated in religion and morals, he appointed for us and the synod itself, to which he imposed and committed, inflamed with zeal of devotion, that the doctrine of the faith, which the holy Roman church holds and preaches, in the name of his patriarch and he would reverently receive from his fellow Jacobins, to be conveyed afterwards by him to the patriarch himself and the Jacobins, so that they too might recognize the same rate which they had and preach in their regions.

We, therefore, who by the voice of the Lord have been commissioned to feed Christ's sheep (Cf. John 21:17), caused Andrew the abbot himself to be carefully examined by some distinguished men of this sacred council on the articles of faith and the sacraments of the church, and on those concerning salvation, and finally, as far as we saw fit it would be necessary, having been expounded to the same abbot in the holy Roman Church in the Catholic faith and humbly accepted by him, this following, true and necessary doctrine we delivered today in this solemn session to the sacred and approving Ecumenical Council of Florence in the name of the Lord.

Therefore, first of all, the sacred Roman Church, founded on the voice of our Lord and Savior, firmly believes, professes and preaches the one true God, omnipotent, immutable and eternal; the Father and the Son and the Holy Spirit; one in essence, triune in persons, begotten of the Father, the Son begotten of the Father, the Holy Spirit proceeding from the Father and the Son, the Father not being the Son or the Holy Spirit, the Son not being the Father or the Holy Spirit, the Holy Spirit not being the Father or the Son, but the Father only the Father is, only the Son is the Son, only the Holy Spirit is the Holy Spirit. The Father alone begot the Son from his own substance. Only the Son is begotten of the Father alone. Only the Holy Spirit proceeds at the same time from the Father and the Son, these three persons are one God, not three gods, because the three are one substance, one essence, one nature, one divinity, one immensity, one eternity, and all are one, where there is no overlap of relation opposition Because of this unity the Father is all in the Son, all in the Holy Spirit, the Son is all in the Father, all in the Holy Spirit, the Holy Spirit is all in the Father, all in the Son. No one else either precedes in eternity or exceeds in greatness or surpasses in power. For it is eternal and without beginning that the Son proceeded from the Father, and it is eternal and without beginning that the Holy Spirit proceeds from the Father to the Son. Whatever the Father is or has, he does not have from another, but from himself, and is the beginning without a beginning. Whatever the Son is or has, he has from the Father, and is the beginning of the beginning. Whatever the Holy Spirit is or has, it has from the Father and the Son together. But the Father and the Son are not two principles of the Holy Spirit, but one principle, just as the Father and the Son and the Holy Spirit are not three principles in the creature, but one principle.

Therefore, he condemns, reprobates and anathematizes all those who feel contrary and contrary, and denounces them as aliens from the body of Christ, which is the church. Hence, he condemns Sabellius, who confuses the persons and completely removes their real distinction; he condemns the Arians, Eunomians, and Macedonians, who say that the Father alone is the true God, but place the Son and the Holy Spirit in the order of creatures. He also condemns any others who have degrees or inequalities in the Trinity.

He firmly believes, professes, and preaches that there is one true God, the Father, the Son, and the Holy Spirit, the creator of all things visible and invisible, who, when he willed, created all creatures, both spiritual and corporeal, by his goodness; they are made of nothing, there is no nature that is evil, because all nature, in so far as it is nature, is good.

He professes one and the same God of the old and new testaments, that is, the author of the law and of the prophets and of the gospel, because by the same Holy Spirit the saints of both testaments spoke, whose books he receives and venerates which are contained in the following titles. The five of Moses are Genesis, Exodus, Leviticus, Numbers, and Deuteronomy; Joshua, Judges, Ruth, Four Kings, Two Chronicles, Ezra, Nehemiah, Tobias, Judith, Hester, Job, Psalms, David, Parables, Ecclesiastes, Song of Songs, Wisdom, Ecclesiastes, Isaya, Jeremiah, Baruch, Ezekiel, Daniel, Twelve For the Minor Prophets, that is Hosea, Joel, Amos, Obadiah, Jonah, Micah, Nahum, Habakkuk, Zephaniah, Haggai, Zechariah, Malachi; two Maccabees, in the Four Gospels, Matthew, Mark, Luke, and John; The fourteen epistles of Paul, to the Romans, two to the Corinthians, to the Galatians, to the Ephesians, to the Philippians, two to the Thessalonians, to the Colossians, two to Timothy, to Titus, to Philemon, to the Hebrews; Peter (albeit doubtful); John's tribe; One of James; One of Jude; the Acts of the Apostles, and in the Apocalypse of John.

Therefore, he anathematizes the madness of the Manichaeans, who established two first principles, one of the visible, the other of the invisible, and said that one was the God of the New Testament, another of the old.

He firmly believes, professes, and preaches one person of the Trinity, the true God, the Son of God, begotten of the Father, consubstantial and coeternal with the Father, in the fullness of time, which the divine plan in the inscrutable height arranged, for the sake of the salvation of the human race, the true whole of man whose nature came from the immaculate womb of the virgin Mary that he assumed and joined himself in unity in the person of such a unity, that whatever is there of God is not separated from man, and whatever is of man is not divided from deity, that one and the same indivisible, both natures are permanent in their properties, God and man, the Son of God and the Son of man, equal to the Father in terms of divinity, inferior to the Father in terms of humanity (the Athanasian Symbol), immortal and eternal by the nature of divinity, passable and temporal by the assumed condition of humanity.

He firmly believes, confesses and preaches that the Son of God was truly born of a virgin in assumed humanity, truly suffered, truly died and was buried, truly rose from the dead, ascended into heaven, and sits at the right hand of the Father, and will come at the end of the ages to judge the living and the dead. And he anathematizes, curses, and condemns every heretic who opposes the wise. And first he condemns Ebion, Cherintus, Marcion, Paulus of Samosata, and Photinus, all who similarly blaspheme, who, not being able to perceive the personal union of humanity with the Word, denied that Jesus Christ our Lord is the true God, confessing himself a pure man, who by divine grace participates in a greater than a more holy one had he accepted life by merit, he would have been called a divine man. He also anathematizes Manicheus with his followers, who, dreaming that the Son of God had taken not a real body, but a fantastic one, completely rejected the truth of humanity in Christ. the water runs over the aqueduct as it flows down. Arius also, asserting that the body taken from a virgin lacked a soul, wished instead of a soul to be a deity. Apollinaris also, who understands that if the soul informing the body is denied, then in Christ there was no true humanity there, he held that the sensitive soul was the only one, but that the deity of the word held the place of the rational soul. He also anathematizes Theodore Mopsuestenus and Nestorius, who affirm that humanity is united to the Son of God by grace, and that for this reason there are two persons in Christ, just as they admit that there are two natures, when they were unable to understand that the union of humanity existed with the hypostatic word, and therefore denied that the word received the subsistence.

LAETENTUR CAELI

For according to this blasphemy, the word was not made flesh, but the word dwelt in the flesh by grace, that is, the Son of God did not become man, but rather the Son of God dwelt in man. He also anathematizes, curses, and condemns the archimandrite Eutychus, who, when he understood, according to the blasphemy of Nestorius, that the truth of the incarnation was excluded, and therefore that it was necessary that humanity should be so united by the word of God, that deity and humanity were one and the same person, and also that he could not grasp the unity of natures in a person, standing in the plurality of natures. as he posited that deity and humanity were one person in Christ, so he asserted that there was one nature, willing that before the union there had been a duality of natures, but that they had passed into one nature in the assumption, conceding the greatest blasphemy and impiety, or that humanity was converted into deity or deity into humanity. He also anathematizes, execrates, and condemns Macharius of Antiochene all such wise men, who, although he truly felt the duality of natures and the unity of the person, nevertheless erred enormously in regard to the operations of Christ, saying that in Christ there was one operation, and one will in the nature of both. The sacred Roman Church anathematizes all these with her heretics, affirming that in Christ there are two wills and two operations.

He firmly believes, professes and teaches that no one who was conceived in a man and a woman has ever been freed from the dominion of the devil, except through the faith of the mediator of God and men, Jesus Christ (1 Tim. 2:5), our Lord, who was born without sin and died the enemy of the human race , by blotting out our sins, he alone prostrated himself with his death, and opened the entrance to the heavenly kingdom, which the first man had lost through his own sin with all succession, which all the sacred sacrifices, sacraments, and ceremonies of the Old Testament foretold that he would one day come.

He firmly believes, professes, and teaches the laws of the Old Testament, or the Mosaic Law, which are divided into ceremonies, sacred sacrifices, and sacraments, because they were instituted for the sake of signifying some future grace, although they corresponded to the divine worship of that age, and it is signified by them that it ceased with the coming of our Lord Jesus Christ, and the new having received the sacraments of the testament. Whoever, even after suffering, puts his hope in the laws and persuades himself to them as if they were necessary for salvation, as if the faith of Christ could not save without them, has sinned mortally. However, he does not deny that they could have been preserved from Christ's passion until the gospel was proclaimed, although they would not have been considered necessary for salvation. But after the proclamation of the gospel, without the destruction of salvation, he asserts that it cannot be preserved eternally.

All, then, after that period of circumcision and the rest of the sabbath, which the observant of the law declares to be strangers to the faith of Christ, and eternal salvation cannot at all be partakers, unless they at some time repent of these errors. Therefore, to all who boast of the Christian name, he absolutely commands that at any time, either before or after baptism, circumcision ceases, because whether one places hope in it or not, it cannot be observed at all without the destruction of eternal salvation. But with regard to children, because of the danger of death which may befall the fence, when they cannot be helped by any other remedy than by the sacrament of baptism, by which they are delivered from the dominion of the devil and are adopted as children of God, he advises that they should not be for forty or eighty days, or any other period according to certain observances. holy baptism should be postponed, but should be conferred as soon as conveniently possible, even so that, in imminent danger of death, they should be baptized soon without any delay, even by a layman or a woman, in the form of a church, if a priest is wanting, as is more fully contained in the decree of the Armenians.

He firmly believes, confesses and preaches that every creature of God is good, nothing to be rejected, which is perceived with thanksgiving (1 Tim. 4:4), because according to the word of the Lord, not what enters the mouth defiles a man (Mt. 15:11), and that according to the Mosaic Law of worldly foods and He asserts that the difference of the unclean belongs to the ceremonials, which passed away with the rising of the gospel and ceased to be effective. He also says that the prohibition of the apostles, being suffocated by sacrificial images and blood (Acts. 15:29), coincided with that time when the church arose out of the Jews and the Gentiles, who formerly lived in different ceremonies and manners, so that the Jews and the Gentiles also had something in common. they should observe and believe in the one worship of God, that the occasion of meeting should be given, and the matter of dissension removed, whereas to the Jews,

LAETENTUR CAELI

because of the ancient custom, blood and strangled were seen as abominable, and by the eating of immolations they might think that the Gentiles would return to idolatry. But when the Christian religion had spread so far, that no carnal Jew appeared in it, but all passing to the church for the same rites of the gospel as they should meet, believing all things to be pure and clean (Titus 1:15), the effect of that apostolic prohibition ceasing to cease also ceased. He declares, therefore, that no nature of food is to be condemned, which human society admits, nor that any distinction should be made between animals by whom, whether male or female, and by whatever kind of death they may die, although for the health of the body, for the exercise of virtue, for regular and ecclesiastical discipline, many things may and should be allowed without denying; because according to the apostle all things are lawful but not all things are expedient (1 Cor. 6:12; 10:22).

He firmly believes, confesses and preaches that no one outside the Catholic Church, not only pagans, but neither Jews nor heretics and schismatics, can become partakers of eternal life, but will go into eternal fire, which is prepared for the devil and his angels (Mt. 25:41), unless before the end they were united to the same life, so much so that the unity of the body of the ecclesiastic should be strong, so that those who remain in it alone may perform the ecclesiastical sacraments for salvation, and fasting, almsgiving, and other acts of piety and exercises in Christian warfare may yield eternal rewards; who has shed blood in his name, can be saved, unless he remains in the bosom and unity of the Catholic Church.

And he embraces, approves, and accepts the holy Nicene Synod of three hundred and eighteen fathers assembled in the time of the blessed Sylvester our predecessor and the great pious prince Constantine, in which the impious Arian heresy was condemned with its author, and it was defined that the Son of God is consubstantial and coeternal with the Father.

He also embraces, approves, and receives the holy Constantinople synod of one hundred and fifty fathers, convened in the time of our most blessed predecessor Damasus and Theodosius the Elder, who anathematized the impious Macedonian error, which asserted that the Holy Spirit is not God, but a

LAETENTUR CAELI

creature. Whom they condemn, he condemns, what they approve, he approves, and throughout everything he wishes to remain there undefined, unharmed and inviolable.

He also embraces, approves, and accepts the holy first Ephesian synod of the two hundred fathers, which is the third in the order of universal synods, convened under the most blessed Celestine our predecessor and Theodosius the younger, in which the impious Nestorius was condemned for blasphemy, which is defined as our Lord Jesus Christ, the true God and truth that there is one person of man, and that the blessed Mary, ever virgin, is not only Christotochon, but also theotochum; this is to be preached by every church, not only as the mother of man, but of God.

He condemns, anathematizes, and rejects the impious Second Synod of Ephesus, assembled under our most blessed Leo, our predecessor and the aforesaid prince, in which Dioscorus the Alexandrian, the defender of Eutychus the heresiarch and the impious persecutor of Saint Flavian, the pontiff of Constantinople, drew that execrable synod to the approval of Eutychus' impiety by art and threats.

He also embraces, approves, and receives the holy synod of Chalcedon, the fourth in the order of universal synods, celebrated in the time of the aforesaid most blessed Leo, our predecessor and Martian prince, the fourth in the order of universal synods, six hundred and thirty, in which the Eutician heresy was condemned with its author Eutyces and Dioscorus the defender, and our master was defined That Jesus Christ is true God and true in name, and in one and the same person as a divine human being with whole, inviolable, uncorrupted, unconfused, distinct natures, that he remained in active humanity, which is man's, and in deity, which is God's. Those whom he condemns, he has condemned; those whom he approves are approved.

He also embraces, approves, and accepts the second holy fifth synod at Constantinople, celebrated at the time of the blessed Vigil of our predecessor and prince Justinian, in which the definition of the sacred Council of

LAETENTUR CAELI

Chalcedon concerning the two natures and one person of Christ was renewed, and the many errors of Origen, his followers, especially concerning the demons of others who penance and deliverance of the condemned, rejected and condemned.

He also embraces, approves, and receives the holy third Constantinople synod of one hundred and fifty fathers, which is the sixth in the order of universal synods, assembled in the times of the most blessed Agathon our predecessor and of Constantine IV, the prince of this name, in which the heresy of Macarius of Antiochene and his followers was condemned, and it was defined in our Lord In Jesus Christ there were two perfect and whole natures and two operations, two wills also, although he was one and the same person, to whom the actions of both belonged by nature, the active deity, which are God's, and the humanity, which are man's.

He also embraces, approves, and accepts all other universal synods legitimately assembled, celebrated, and confirmed by the authority of the Roman Pontiff, and especially this holy Florentine one, in which, among other things, the most holy union of the Greeks and Armenians was consummated, and many salutary definitions were published concerning both unions, as in it is fully contained in the decrees promulgated above, the tenor of which follows in this manner.

Rejoice in heaven [...]

Shout out to God [...]

It is true that in the above-mentioned decree of the Armenians the form of the word rum is not explained, which in the consecration of the body and blood of the Lord the sacred Roman church, established by the teaching and authority of the apostles Peter and Paul, has always been accustomed to use, we have decided to insert it in the present. In the consecration of the Lord's body, he uses this form of words: For this is my body. For this is the cup of my blood, of the new and eternal testament, the mystery of faith, which will be poured out for you and for many for the remission of sins (Mt 26,28; Mk 14,18; Lk 22,10; 1 Cor 11,25).

Now the wheaten bread, in which the sacrament is made, whether it was boiled on that day or earlier, makes no difference at all; for as long as the substance of the bread remains, there is no doubt whatsoever that after the aforementioned words of consecration of the body, uttered by the priest with the intention of making it, it will soon be transubstantiated into the true body of Christ.

Because some are said to reject fourth marriages as condemned, lest it should be thought that there is sin where there is none, when, according to the apostle, a woman is freed from the law of a dead husband and has the ability in the Lord to marry whom she wills (Rm. 7:3; 1 Cor. 7). We say, however, that it is more commendable if they continue in chastity, abstaining from marriage, because virginity is to widowhood, so we consider that chaste widowhood is to be preferred to marriage with praise and merit.

Having explained all these things, the aforesaid Andrew the abbot, in the name of the said patriarch and proper and of all the Jacobins, this most salutary synodal decree with all its chapters, declarations, definitions, traditions, precepts and statutes, and all the doctrine described in it, as well as whatever the holy apostolic see and the Roman church holds and teaches, with he receives and accepts it with all devotion and reverence. Those teachers and holy fathers whom the Roman church approves, he himself reverently receives; indeed, whatever persons and whatever the Roman Church itself reproves and condemns; He himself has for the reprobate and damned, professing as in true obedience to the name of the Son, above, faithfully and always to obey the ordinances and commands of his apostolic see.

Having solemnly read this decree in the present synod, in Latin, then in Arabic, the aforesaid Andrew, the abbot, publicly read the decree of the Jacobins themselves there, and added the following words written in Arabic, which were recited to the incontinent: most blessed father…

LAETENTUR CAELI

[...]

Given at Florence in a public synodal session, solemnly celebrated in the church of the house of St. Maria Novella, where we now reside, in the year of the Incarnation Sunday 1442, the day before the ninth of February, in the year 10 of our pontificate.

He gives on February 4, 1441, in the 10th year of his Pontificate.

The Scriptorium Project is the work of a small group of lay people of various apostolic churches who are interested in the preservation, transmission, and translation of the works of the early and medieval church. Our efforts are to make the works of the church fathers accessible to anyone who might have an interest in Christian antiquities and the theological, philosophical, and moral writings that have become the bedrock of Western Civilization.

To-date, our releases have pulled from the Greek, Syriac, Georgian, Latin, Celtic, Ethiopian, and Coptic traditions of Christianity, and have been pulled from sundry local traditions and languages.

www.ingramcontent.com/pod-product-compliance
Lightning Source LLC
LaVergne TN
LVHW051922060526
838201LV00060B/4141